HTML5 Development:
The Beginning Beginners Guide
Getting started in HTML5 with absolutely no experience

By

Jason Pfaff

LearnToProgram Media

Vernon, Connecticut

LearnToProgram.tv, Incorporated
27 Hartford Turnpike Suite 206
Vernon, CT 06066

contact@learntoprogram.tv

(860) 840-7090

ISBN-13: 978-0692619711
ISBN-10: 0692619712
©2016 by LearnToProgram.tv, Incorporated

About the App Development Guide series

The App Development Guide series from LearnToProgram Media is designed to provide you with guides for creating interesting apps. The app development guides provide all of the code, assets, and other materials that you will need to create complete applications. Some of the apps in this series are designed to work within a web browser while others are designed to be deployed to mobile devices—either as a native iOS or Android App or as a HTML5 based app that works on both platforms.

The best way to learn app development is to actually build apps. Our goal is not to provide an exhaustive explanation for every tag, method and property we use in building the apps. In this series, it is our hope that the guides will provide context to integrate what you've learned previously, and, perhaps, set you up for future learning.

I hope that you gain a great deal of satisfaction from coding along with these guides and making the app work on your own. Once the app is working I'd invite you to modify the app—add features and make it more interesting, usable or useful.

I am a big believer in the learn-by-doing paradigm—it is how I gained much of the skillset I boast today. I hope after working through our App Development Guide series, that you will feel the same.

If you have any feedback about any of the books in this series, please don't hesitate to reach out to me at mark@learntoprogram.tv or @mlassoff on Twitter.

Technologies

This app development guide uses the following technologies:

- HTML5
- CSS

The final application may be fun on any contemporary Mac or PC with a current browser.

Assets and Code

All of the assets and code for this book are available to you at
https://learntoprogram.tv/pages/request-book-assets. Simply provide
your email address as directed and you will receive a link to the assets
and code via email in just a few minutes.

Table of Contents

Introduction

Congratulations! You have taken an important first step on what will be a fun and memorable journey as you learn HTML5 and begin to create your very own web pages. This should feel empowering. You understand how much joy and fun your favorite websites bring you. Our goal with this book is to take you step by step through the process that will enable you to build creative and fun sites that give your visitors the same experience.

The secret of the modern web is that anyone can learn to build and create fun and informative sites. And you can have as much fun building the site as visitors have exploring it!

This book is designed with you, the beginner, in mind. We will work through simple examples together step by step and start at the absolute beginning. Our goal is to provide an engaging look at each step so that you build knowledge and confidence as we go. Our commitment is that you will build the skills and understanding that will allow you to create your own sites in a way that allows you to understand, and then learn by doing.

Let's build!

The Building Blocks of HTML5: Elements, Tags, and Attributes

If you have ever looked at HTML5 before or tried to build a website, you might feel like it is akin to rocket science and that it is complicated and intimidating. Our hope is that as you proceed through this book, the feeling of intimidation will melt away and you will gain meaningful confidence in your ability to build pages for the World Wide Web.

The best place to start building confidence is with a very brief understanding of what HTML5 is and what it is used for.

At its simplest, HTML5 is a language used for structuring and presenting content on the World Wide Web. The goal of any website is communication. Your HTML5 code will structure, format and then work with a browser to present your content to communicate with your visitors. The current standard, HTML5, is the most current standard of the language. HTML is constantly evolving to support the latest in multimedia and technology. This is good news for you as the language remains current and flexible allowing you to communicate your content on the latest devices and in ways that are important to you.

Most of the additional styling and design elements that infuse web pages come from another language, CSS or Cascading Style Sheet language. We will briefly touch on CSS in this book, but a deeper review of CSS is beyond our scope. We will mainly focus on the basic HTML5 elements of a webpage, so that a browser can read your page and deliver it to your visitors.

The first step to learning a simple approach to HTML5 and building pages for the web is to understand how simple the building blocks actually are. The basic building blocks of all HTML5 programs are elements, tags, and attributes. The foundation of your program will be your HTML elements, and your tags and attributes are parts of your elements that give you control over the content, layout and structure of your content and ultimately, your site.

Here is an example of tags. I have highlighted them in the example:

<p>This is text that will appear on a website</p>

We will cover many types of tags and what they mean later in the book. In this case, <p> is short for paragraph, and the text between the bracketed tags will appear in the browser. It is not necessary to what about what the tags do yet. It is more important to focus on the overall structure.

Element

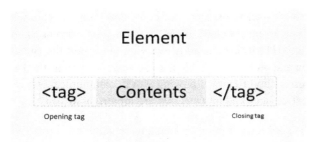

Figure 1-1—HTML elements and tags

Tags are always bookended by angle brackets. The letters inside the brackets indicate the type of tag it is. The contents of the tag represent the content that the tag is structuring for a browser. Most tags have a closing tag which is symbolized by a forward slash in front of the tag name inside of the normal angle brackets.

It might be necessary to add additional content or structure with a tag. We do that using an attribute.

Here is our example tag we used previously. However, now we have added an attribute. I have highlighted the attribute.

This is text that will appear on a website

As you can probably guess, the attribute, in this case, will center our text.

An attribute is placed within the opening tag and an HTML tag can have one or many attributes. Attributes are always included in the opening tag. They are preceded by a space and they include the name of the attribute, an equal sign, and a value in quotes.

Figure 1-2—Placement of an attribute

With that as a base of understanding, I am confident you are ready to write your first lines of HTML5 code! There is only one additional tool that we need.

One of the most basic tools for building a web page is a text editor. A text editor will not only house your code but it will also help you keep your web page project organized. A good text editor is your best friend when you build code for your sites.

There are many available options for very good text editors. For this project, we will use Brackets from Adobe. Brackets is a great editor, easy to install, and simple to use. However, do not let its simplicity fool you. It also has very powerful capabilities and is used every day by many professionals building and maintaining the websites of tomorrow.

The first step is to download and install your text editor.

How to install and run Brackets:

Figure 1-2.5—Download screen for Brackets.io

1. In your browser, navigate to Brackets.io and click on the blue download button in the middle of the screen that says "Download Brackets".

2. Click Open to open the Installer.

3. Follow the instructions on the installer and click finish or install.

4. When you are finished with the installation, open Brackets.

5. By default, Brackets opens a folder containing some simple "Getting Started" content. Read through this to get a feel for Brackets and some of the

terminology used. Don't worry if you don't
understand some or all of what it covers.

Your First Program

Now that you have access to Brackets, it is time to build your first
HTML5 script! Let me be the first to congratulate you. In the next few
minutes, you will have your very first page up.

Your first step is to create a new folder where you would like to save
your files and store your webpage.

1. Right click in the location you want to create your folder such as
your desktop or normal folder directory

2. Click "New"

3. Click "Folder".

4. Name your folder My Page.

Now that you have a project folder created, it is time to start a file in
your text editor. In Brackets, click "File" and then "New".

At this point, you have a blank text file in the text editor. This is exactly
where every good web page starts.

Let's type our first line of text into Brackets for our site. I'll start with:

Thanks for visiting my page and learning more about me!

After typing this, follow this simple process to start saving your file.

1. Click "File"

2. Click "Save as"

3. Name your first page index.html

It is critical to use a .html extension so that your text editor and browsers know to read this file as an HTML file. The title index is a customary title for the primary or home page of a website. For the purposes of this exercise, I'll save our first page as:

index.html

Now click "Save". At this point, you should have your very first page to render to a browser. In Brackets, you will click on the small lightning bolt icon in the upper right of your screen to test your code in a browser. This is called the Live Preview feature.

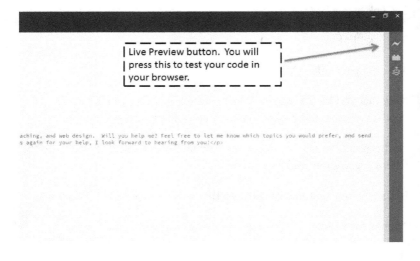

Figure 1-3—Live Preview feature in Brackets

If you do this now, you should see this:

Figure 1-4—First rendering to browser

Congratulations! This is the small and humble starting point of what will be a fantastic web page in the not so distant future. All web pages start as a blank canvas.

From this first step, we can see that we are able to render content to a browser with no additional HTML5. This will remain true throughout all of your scripts. Your text and other parts of your content will maintain their native structure. The HTML tags and attributes that you place around your content will assist you in building a web page by structuring that content. Additionally, a great deal of styling, design and decorative elements will come from the CSS you add.

Let's delete the first line we typed that we used as a test. We will now add some basic HTML tags and begin to build our actual site. We will add the tags below to our index.html file in Brackets. This is known as the HTML Boilerplate. It is the initial starting point for every page built in HTML.

Code sample: Initial HTML Boilerplate

```
<!DOCTYPE html>
```

```
<html>
<head>
<title></title>
</head>
<body>
</body>
</html>
```

The !DOCTYPE declaration indicates to the browser the version of HTML that the document is written in. Every HTML file you write will have the same starting point. It must be there and it must always be on top.

The first tag <html> simply tells the browser that an HTML file is being delivered and will need to be rendered.

The <head> tag acts as a container or place for content like titles and meta data that would normally go in the "head" or top of a document.

The <html> tags indicate the start and end of an HTML5 document. The text after the <title> tag will appear in the browser tab while the page is open. The title tag content is also used by search engines such as Google to index your site once it is launched on the web. The </title> closes that portion of the document and the </head> closes out the header section.

The <body> tag will act as a container for elements like paragraphs and images that typically appear in the body of a webpage.

The </body> tag closes out that section, and the </html> signals the end of the document.

After typing in the boilerplate above, your code in your text editor should look like the image below:

Figure 1-5—HTML boilerplate in Brackets editor

As a general rule, all tags which contain content will have both opening and closing tags. There are some tags which do not include or require closing tags, but they are beyond our current scope.

Now that we have our boilerplate, we need to determine the objective of our page, grab a few ideas, and then it is time to start building!

For our project, we will build a site to serve as a personal profile. It will provide a basic layout to a page that will contain personal details, images, links to favorite sites, information about work history, and a place for feedback from our visitors.

I will make up personal details about a fictional person and provide the basic structure for a personal profile type website. Feel free to add your details as we go in the text portions, but please ensure that you are following the code exactly.

The first step is to name our page. Between the <title> opening and closing tags, I will put "My page", which will serve as our title.

In the <body> section, I will put text welcoming our visitors.

Your code should now resemble what is shown below:

Code Sample: Adding initial content

```
<!DOCTYPE html>
<html>
<head>
        <title>My Page</title>
</head>
<body>
Thanks for visiting my page and learning more about me!
</body>
</html>
```

Adding Basic Tags for Formatting and Styling

Now that we have some basic text and our boilerplate, it is time to add several tags to help you structure text elements and to build the majority of the content on your page.

The secret is that many web pages require only a handful of tags for the majority of their content. Understanding the purpose, functionality and best uses of the basic tags will accelerate your ability to build fun and creative web pages that are filled with interesting and relevant content structured exactly the way you want it.

Two of the most common tags that you will use are header and paragraph tags. Header options number 1 through 6 with one typically being the primary header and subsequent headers decreasing in importance as the numbers get larger. The primary header opening tag is <h1> and the closing tag is </h1>. The secondary header opening tag will look like <h2> with the customary closing syntax of </h2>. You will follow the same pattern with subsequent headers, although most pages rarely go as far as <h5> or <h6>.

Let's create our header tag. These tags are important to your visitors and will help them with navigation. Great web pages are intuitive and easy to navigate because they were built with strong visual cues and elements like headers. I will add <h1> tags around my existing text so that it has more emphasis. I have highlighted the new code below to add to our boilerplate:

Code Sample: Adding a header

```
<!DOCTYPE html>
<html>
<head>
<title>My Page</title>
</head>
<body>
<h1>Thanks for visiting my page and learning more about me!</h1>
</body>
</html>
```

Save your code and click on Live Preview in your text editor to test it in the browser. Notice the difference before and after you added the <h1> tags.

When viewed in the browser, your page should now resemble this image:

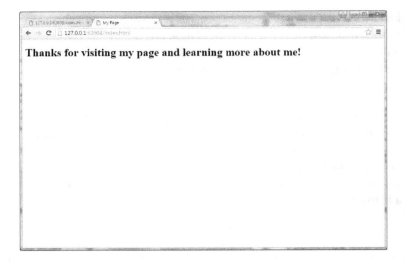

Figure 1-6—The addition of header tags

Congratulations on making it so far! By understanding the placement and importance of basic tags, you are learning the routine that it takes to build web pages. If it takes you a few tries, no worries! You will find that a great deal of coding is trial and error and even the most experienced and skilled programmers work this way. The key is to keep progressing forward, learn as much as you can, look for creative ways to solve problems and apply new lessons as quickly as possible.

Another very common tag that you will often use is the paragraph, or <p> tag. Most of the text based content on your site will live between opening <p> and closing </p> tags.

Knowing we are building a personal profile web page, I have added some brief biographical information between the <p> tags in our <body> section that we can build on in later lessons.

I have highlighted the code and text I added in the following example.

Code Sample: Adding a paragraph tag

```
<!DOCTYPE html>
<html>
<head>
<title>My Page</title>
</head>
<body>
<h1> Thanks for visiting my page and learning more about me!
</h1>
<p>I graduated from the University of Texas in 2010 with a degree
in English.  I am an English teacher and soccer coach and
learning to build web pages.</p>
</body>
</html>
```

After entering the <p> tags, save and test your code in a browser. The
following screen shot demonstrates how my page is rendering.

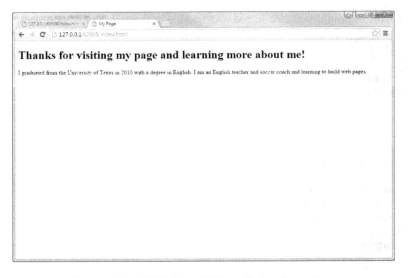

Figure 1-7—With the addition of a header and <p> tags

Let's add a secondary header to provide a visual and navigational cue to visitors as to what to expect with the page. I am going to add an <h2> tag and some text which is replicated and highlighted in the code sample below.

Code Sample: Adding a secondary header tag

```
<!DOCTYPE html>
<html>
<head>
<title>My Page</title>
</head>
<body>
<h1>Thanks for visiting my page and learning more about me! </h1>
```

```
<h2>This site is designed as a personal profile</h2>
<p>I graduated from the University of Texas in 2010 with a degree
in English.  I am an English teacher and soccer coach and
learning to build web pages.</p>
</body>
</html>
```

We should now have a page title, two headers, and some content in a paragraph tag. We should make sure that we save our file. When we click on the live preview icon in Brackets, we should see the following render in a browser:

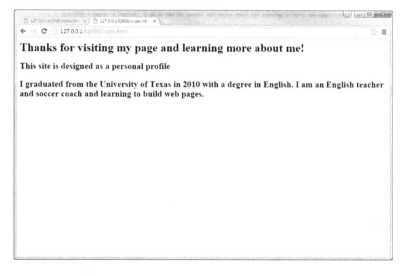

Figure 1-8—With the addition of a secondary header

Fantastic progress! I trust you feel empowered to continue now that we have some basic foundational pieces in place to build our site around.

The Supporting Cast for Your HTML

It is exciting to reflect on the progress that we have made thus far. We are building the foundation of a great website with solid code and great content. As we mentioned earlier, great content is the heart of any meaningful website, and good HTML code provides the structure, organization, and layout for your content.

However, a lot more goes into delivering a quality website, and now we are going to discuss three important supporting pieces; the browser, text editor, and cascading style sheets (CSS) for introducing styling.

The web browser is the software application that your visitors will use to access and view your site. Browsers access, navigate and present the information and content that makes up the World Wide Web. As you begin to build and place content on the web for popular consumption, it will be important to stay mindful of the critical role that browsers play. A major part of why we want to properly use tags and keep our code organized is so that browsers can easily navigate and understand our pages, and properly display them.

As you are probably aware, there are several main choices for browsers today. Chrome, Safari, Firefox, and Internet Explorer are the most commonly used browsers. Well organized code with accurate tags will perform well in browsers and render the intended structure and format for your content.

The main tool we use to keep our code organized, structured and functioning well is a text editor. The text editor that we have chosen here is Brackets.io, which is an open source project sponsored by Adobe.

Just like your visitors have several choices of browsers to use to visit your page, you ultimately have many choices when it comes to text editors. Several common options include Notepad++, TextMate, and Sublime Text. Different editors will have different functionalities and interfaces, but most often, web designers and developers choose a text editor based on personal preferences. They usually stick with an editor that they enjoy using.

One very helpful and common way of using a text editor to ensure that you keep your code organized is through the use of comments. In the context of coding, comments are helpful notes that you write to yourself or others who will read your code. These notes are embedded within the code, but they are written with a certain syntax that will prevent them from being read with the rest of your HTML. In addition, they will not interfere with how your page is rendered in the browser. You can think of comments as having their own tag, which is provided in the example below.

Code Sample: The comment tag and adding comments

```
<!--This is a comment. Comments are not displayed in the browser-->

<p>This is a paragraph. This will be displayed in the browser.</p>
```

In Brackets. (and several other text editors) there is a simple keyboard shortcut to work with comments. Simply highlight the area you want to comment and press Ctrl and / (Command and / on a Mac) at the same time. You should see the comment tags appear and your text in that section should turn gray. There will be times where you want to "comment out" code as you are working back and forth with page designs. Let's say that after adding our secondary header tag, you want to look at the page with and without the header. Here is how our page currently renders:

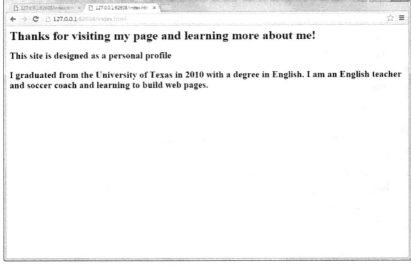

Figure 2-1—Current version of page

Now, let's "comment out" our <h2> tag. I will highlight that <h2> tag with my cursor, and press Ctrl + /

I have highlighted in yellow, the line we are commenting out in the code sample below.

Code Sample: Commenting out a line of code

```
<h1>Thanks for visiting my page and learning more about me!</h1>
<!--<h2>This site is designed as a personal profile<h2>-->
</head>
```

```
<body>
<p>I graduated from the University of Texas in 2010 with a degree
in English.  I am an English teacher and soccer coach and
learning to build web pages.</p>
```

When we now render our page to the browser, you will notice it simply removed that line of code from what it renders to the browser:

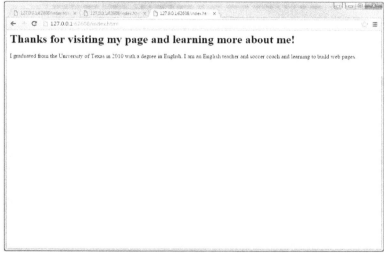

Figure 2-2—Results from commenting out a line of code

Now that we have looked at our page without the header, we want to return it to the content visitors will see in the browser. We need to remove the comment from our code. To do this, we will simply highlight the code we want to remove the comment tags from, in this case our <h2> tags, and press Ctrl + / again. After doing this, our code should look like the following sample.

Code Sample: Uncommenting out a line of code

```
<!DOCTYPE html>
<html>
<head>
<title>My Page</title>
</head>

<body>
<h1>Thanks for visiting my page and learning more about me! </h1>

<h2>This site is designed as a personal profile.</h2>

<p> I graduated from the University of Texas in 2010 with a
degree in English.  I am an English teacher and soccer coach and
learning to build web pages.</p>
</body>
</html>
```

Congratulations! You are now developing skills used every day by professional developers. The ability to use comments and understand the role of browsers and text editors will serve you well on this project and beyond as you build fun, exciting and creative web pages.

CSS : Adding a sense of style to your page

One of the best parts of building web pages is that it offers both an opportunity to work in a standard format which anyone can learn. At the same time, it offers a great deal of flexibility and options to build design elements which give everyone a chance to reflect their own content communicated in a way that is not only effective, but also creative and engaging.

Many of the design features and styling that you see on the web today comes from Cascading Style Sheets, or CSS. As mentioned earlier in the book, HTML structures and formats what you want to communicate and CSS helps you style and present it.

A deep explanation and exploration of CSS is beyond the scope of this book, but I did want to introduce it so you are familiar with how CSS rules are structured, and how you will add CSS style sheets to your HTML documents.

You will build your CSS in a separate file that you will link to your HTML file. This process is very simple, and only requires you to open a new file in your text editor and to add one line of code to the top of your HTML file. Here are the first three steps.

1.   In your My_Page folder, create a new sub-folder and call it CSS.

2.   Open a new file in your text editor and save it with the filename style.css.

3.   Save that file to your new CSS folder inside of your My_Page project.

It is important that you save your file with a .css extension and that you save it to a sub-folder named CSS that is located within your main My_Page project folder.

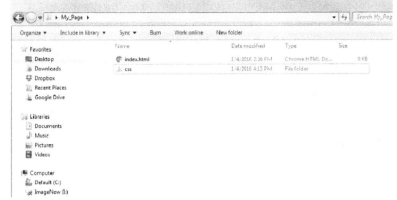

Figure 3-1—Creating a new CSS file

To add our style sheet, we now need to link our CSS to our HTML file. I have titled my style sheet "style.css", so I will use that in my code to link the two.

In the <head> element of your HTML file, you will add a simple line of code to link the two files. Here is sample code for a file named style.css that is housed in a folder named CSS:

Code Sample: Linking CSS to an HTML doc

```
<link rel="stylesheet" type="text/css" href="css/style.css">
```

The code to link the CSS file and the HTML file should be placed towards the top of your HTML file like this:

Code Sample: Adding a CSS rule

```
<!DOCTYPE html>
```

```
<html>
<head>
<title>My Page</title>
<link rel="stylesheet" type="text/css" href="css/style.css">
</head>
<body>
<h1> Thanks for visiting my page and learning more about me!
</h1>
<h2>This site is designed as a personal profile</h2>
<p>I graduated from the University of Texas in 2010 with a degree
in English.  I am an English teacher and soccer coach and
learning to build web pages.</p>
</body>
</html>
```

When you add this code and click save on both files, the two files will be linked. Make sure that both the CSS and HTML files are saved inside of the same project.

CSS will describe to the browser how your HTML elements should be presented. Most commonly, CSS is used to control color, fonts and layout.

While HTML is mostly added through tags, CSS uses what is known as rules. CSS rules generally follow a very simple and standard format which will help you in your ability to begin using them right away.

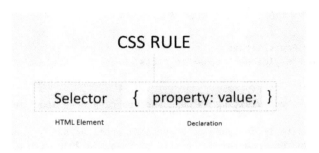

Figure 3-2—Structure of CSS rules

As you can see in the image, CSS rules primarily consist of three basic elements: a selector, property, and value.

The selector is the HTML element that you are styling. For example, if you were styling your primary header, your selector would simply be h1.

The property is the type of style you want to add to it. If you wanted to add text, your property would be color.

The value is the specific nature of that styling that will be applied. This would represent the type or shade of color in our example.

Go ahead and add the code sample shown below to the top of your CSS file.

Code Sample: Adding a CSS rule

```
h1 {
    color: blue;
}
```

At this point, save both your HTML file and CSS sheet and test your code in the browser. It should now have a blue header, just like this!

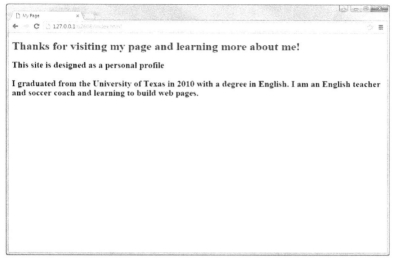

Figure 3-3—Styling text color with our new CSS rule

I hope that you are excited and feel a genuine sense of accomplishment. Adding CSS to your page is fun and helps you add your own unique style. There are many options with fonts and colors and the ways you can use your CSS and HTML together. CSS is a course on its own and I encourage you to continue to pursue learning CSS so that you can get the most out of your web designs.

Let's add one more rule to help us with changing a font, a common use of CSS.

Below your h1 rule, we will add a rule for body indicating the font we want on your CSS sheet.

Code Sample: Adding a CSS rule for font styling

```
body {
    font-family:  Arial, Helvetica, sans-serif

}
```

It is possible to change the font faces with the font-family property. CSS provides several options that make it possible to adjust typography.   The font of all the elements in the body will be changed to Arial., We will use Helvetica as a back-up.Our page should now appear like this:

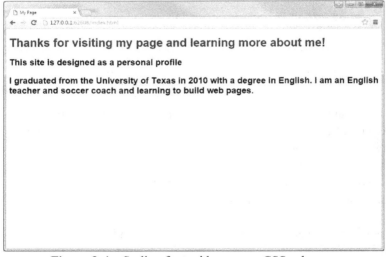

Figure 3-4—Styling font with our new CSS rule

How to present lists of information In its simplest form, a webpage is a vehicle for communicating information. When communicating, it is often helpful to organize certain pieces of information or data into lists. Fortunately, HTML5 provides a very convenient way to accomplish this with the ordered and unordered list elements.

If you are simply bulleting information, and the sequence of the items is not important, you will list items in an unordered list. Unordered lists will have an opening <ul> and closing </ul> tag format that should now be familiar to you.

When we build a list, we will also add tags to each item in the list. The list tags will open <li> and close</li> around each listed item. An easy way to think about this is to consider the <ul> tag as declaring that a list will be built, and each <li> tag is nested within the larger list. Here is a sample of a blank list showing the tags we would use for a three item unordered list:

Code Sample: Adding unordered lists

```
<ul>
  <li></li>
  <li></li>
  <li></li>
</ul>
```

Adding ordered lists, which is a list where items need to have a certain sequence reflected, follows a similar pattern.

However, with an ordered list, we will declare a list with an opening <ol> tag to represent the fact we now want an ordered list. We will close it with a </ol> tag in typical fashion.

We will nest the list items with an ordered list the same way we do with an unordered list. Here is a code sample of a blank ordered list:

Code Sample: Adding an ordered list

```
<ol>
  <li></li>
  <li></li>
  <li></li>
</ol>
```

Now, let's return to our profile page and add some lists! We will head back to where we left off after we added the code to link our style sheet. Your code should look like the below sample:

Code Sample: Current status of code for personal profile project

```
<html>
<head>
        <title>My Page</title>

<link rel="stylesheet" type="text/css" href="css/style.css">
</head>
<body>
<h1>Thanks for visiting my page and learning more about me! </h1>

<h2>This site is designed as a personal profile.</h2>
```

```
<p>I graduated from the University of Texas in 2010 with a degree
in English.  I am an English teacher and soccer coach and
learning to build web pages.</p>
</body>
</html>
```

Let's add some fun details including our interests and hobbies so that
visitors to our page get a sense of our personality. Below our paragraph
element, I am going to add an unordered list with three things that I like
to do in my spare time. I will also add a sentence to my paragraph
element to introduce the list below it. I have highlighted the code that is
new in this step. After adding a sentence to my paragraph element and
an unordered list, my code will now look like this:

Code Sample: Adding an unordered list

```
<html>
<head>
<title>My Page</title>
<link rel="stylesheet" type="text/css" href="css/style.css">
</head>
<body>
<h1>Thanks for visiting my page and learning more about me! </h1>
<h2>This site is designed as a personal profile.</h2>
<p> I graduated from the University of Texas in 2010 with a
degree in English.  I am an English teacher and soccer coach and
learning to build web pages. Here are some things I like to do in
my free time:</p>
<ul>
<li>basketball</li>
<li>soccer </li>
<li>table tennis </li>
</ul>
</body>
```

```
</html>
```

At this point, you will be able to save your file and test your code in the
browser. After doing so, here is what mine looks like:

Figure 4-1—Adding lists

Fantastic work! It looks so good we should add another!

Let's add some professional accomplishments. Due to the nature of the
list, and the fact we want to prioritize what we are most proud of in our
career, we want to list these next elements in order. As we now know,
that calls for an ordered list.

To introduce this list, instead of adding text in a paragraph tag, we will add a new header. Let's add an <h3> to introduce our list, and then nest our list <li> elements inside of our ordered list opening <ol> and closing </ol> tags.

First, I'll add a header indicating to our visitors that we are going to list career accomplishments. We will add this tag right under the unordered list that we just added.

Code Sample: Adding an additional header

```
<h3>Below are some of my career accomplishments</h3>
```

Now we will build our ordered list. These items will be placed in sequence on our page. It should be identical in basic format to our unordered list except for the <ol> tags in place of the <ul> tags. Here is the code that we will place right below the heading tag we just added.

Code Sample: Adding an ordered list

```
<ol>
<li>Teacher of the year in 2011</li>
<li> Coached the Boy's soccer team to the conference title in
2012</li>
<li>Three former students received prestigious scholarships in
2015</li>
</ol>
```

This is excellent progress! We now have headers, a basic style sheet added, some content and two different lists (unordered and ordered).

We have a lot to be proud of! At this point, the code in our text editor on Brackets.io should look like this:

Code Sample: Adding an ordered list

```
<html>
<head>
<title>My Page</title>
<link rel="stylesheet" type="text/css" href="css/style.css">
</head>
<body>
<h1>Thanks for visiting my page and learning more about me! </h1>
<h2>This site is designed as a personal profile.</h2>
<p>I graduated from the University of Texas in 2010 with a degree
in English.  I am an English teacher and soccer coach and
learning to build web pages. Here are some things I like to do in
my free time:</p>
<ul>
<li>basketball</li>
<li> soccer</li>
<li> table tennis</li>
</ul>
<h3> Below are some of my career accomplishments</h3>
<ol>
<li>Teacher of the year in 2011</li>
<li> Coached the Boy's soccer team to the conference title in 201
</li>
<li> Three former students received prestigious scholarships in
2015</li>
</ol>

</body>
</html>
```

Feel free to check your code against the preceding sample and make any necessary adjustments. You might want to take some time at this point to reflect on other ways you can add lists, paragraphs, headers or basic styling with your text in future projects. You should be starting to get a grasp of the functionality available to you as you build your page. This is great! The greatest tool that you have as you build in HTML for the web is your own imagination.

After checking your code against the image above, save it, and then test it in your browser. It should appear like the page below.

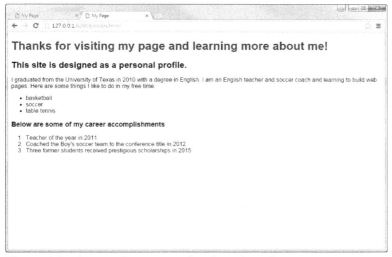

Figure 4-3—Image of current rendered version of our page

As you can see, ordered lists add an additional layer of structure to the ways we can display content on our page. However, this structure is not limiting. As with any HTML element, we have a variety of options for how we want to display lists. Let's look at a few examples!

We may want to start by reversing the order of our items so that the list starts with the highest number and counts down. To structure our list this way, we will add an attribute. Adding attributes is very simple way to provide you with even greater control over how you want to display your content.

If we recall from the first section, an HTML tag can consist of not only the tag name, but also an attribute. Thus far, we have only used tag names, but now it is time to add an attribute. Below is a graphic showing the placement of an attribute.

Figure 4-4—Placement of an attribute

In this case, we want to reverse the order of our ordered list. To accomplish this, we will add the attribute "reversed" to our <ol> tag. Here is a code sample demonstrating how we do this. I have highlighted where I have placed the reverse attribute.

Code Sample: Adding an attribute

```
<ol reversed>
<li>Teacher of the year in 2011</li>we
<li>Coached the Boy's soccer team to the conference title in
2012</li>
<li>Three former students received prestigious scholarships in
2015</li>
```

```
</ol>
```

After adding the code, save your file and test it in the browser. It should render like this:

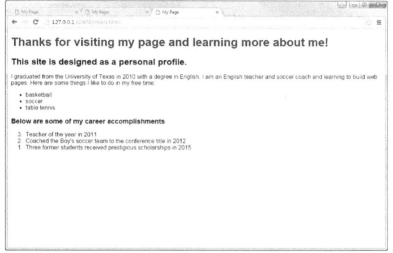

Figure 4-5—Screenshot with our ordered list with reversed attribute

If you prefer letters and an alphabetical display, or if you'd rather use Roman numerals, you have additional options. An ordered list will use traditional decimal numbers by default. But if you would prefer a different symbol, you can declare that as an attribute by indicating the type of symbol you want.

To use uppercase letters alphabetically, you will use the code below. I have highlighted where you add the type:

Code Sample: Adding type to an ordered list

```
<ol type = "A">
<li>Teacher of the year in 2011</li>
<li>Coached the Boy's soccer team to the conference title in
2012</li>
<li>Three former students received prestigious scholarships in
2015</li>
</ol>
```

When you test your code, you should now see your list organized by upper case alphabetical letters. Here is an example:

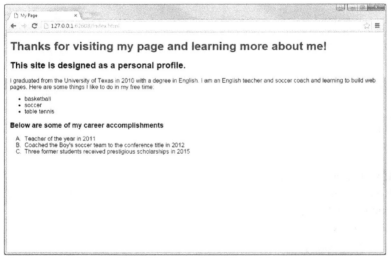

Figure 4-6—Screenshot with our ordered list with type = "A"

To use Roman numerals, you simply add an uppercase "I" to your type declaration. Here is a sample:

Code Sample: Adding type to an ordered list

```
<ol type = "I">
<li>Teacher of the year in 2011</li>
<li>Coached the Boy's soccer team to the conference title in
2012</li>
<li>Three former students received prestigious scholarships in
2015</li>
</ol>
```

To use lowercase letters or Roman numerals, you simply add the lowercase version instead of an uppercase version. Along with our reversed attribute, this allows six different ways that we can display an ordered list. This offers you excellent flexibility and allows you to learn many different ways to structure listed information. An increased understanding of CSS from a future book or course will provide you with many additional styling options for your lists. As a result, your content will not only be well-organized but also creative and engaging.

Links: Connecting to other pages on the World Wide Web

One of the best features of the World Wide Web is the opportunity to easily link many different pages covering a wide variety of information. The convenience of being able to link to other pages provides you many benefits as a site creator. There are many reasons why you might want to add links to your page. We will cover a few of them here. However, I encourage you to use your imagination and think of the numerous ways that you can incorporate links into your web designs. Adding links can support your content and provide a rich, unique and tailored experience to your visitors.

To add a link, you will use an <a> tag with a special attribute. <a> is an abbreviation for anchor. Often, as you will see in the following example, your link tags will live inside of other tags like <h1>, or <p>, or <ul>.

The typical anchor element starts with an opening <a> tag and will have a href attribute. The attribute href is short for hypertext reference. It will have a universal resource locator, or url. This is the website or link address. The second part of the element will have the text that will be rendered to the webpage and contain the link. This means the link text is clickable and houses the url that will take the visitor where they intended to go by clicking on the link.

Here is an example of what a link in HTML looks like:

Code Sample: Basic link structure

```
<a href="url">link text</a>
```

If, for example, I wanted to link to Yahoo.com, I could build the element below.

Code Sample: Basic link structure

```
<a href="http://www.yahoo.com">Click here to go to Yahoo.com</a>
```

Let's look at the process of building a link element. Refer to the preceding code sample, as I outline the steps below.

1. Open the element with an <a tag

2. Add the href= attribute, and then, in quotes, add the url or address for the site you want to link to, exactly as we have done above.

3. Close the link portion with a >

4. Add the text the user will click to activate the link

5. Add a closing </a> tag

While there seems to be more going on in a link element than we have seen in the other elements we have covered thus far, you will always follow the same structure. With a little practice, you will have this new skill mastered and be able to take advantage of the full power of the web by linking to other HTML documents across the world.

Now, let's get more practice by adding a few links to our personal profile. In this section, I will also show you one or two unique functions that can improve the sophistication and functionality of your website.

First, assume that we want to be able to share more information about where we grew up. It would be impractical to add a great deal of information about this since the purpose of this page is to share information about us. However, some visitors might be curious, and might want additional information. By providing them with a link, you can offer them the chance to learn more, while not taking up precious space on your page for those with less interest.

For the purpose of this example, we will say that we grew up in Dallas, Texas and want to add a link to a site providing more information about Dallas.

First, let's start a new biography section to add some of this biographical information. I will start with a new <h3> and then add a brief introduction to the section in a <p> tag. I have highlighted the addition to our full code sample below.

Code Sample: Adding a new header and link

```
<!DOCTYPE html>
<html>
<head>
<title>My Page</title>

<link rel="stylesheet" type="text/css" href="css/style.css">
</head>
<body>
<h1>Thanks for visiting my page and learning more about me! </h1>

<h2>This site is designed as a personal profile.</h2>

<p>I graduated from the University of Texas in 2010 with a degree
in English.  I am an English teacher and soccer coach and
learning to build web pages. Here are some things I like to do in
my free time:</p>

<ul>
<li>basketball</li>
<li> soccer</li>
<li> table tennis</li>
</ul>
<h3> Below are some my career accomplishments</h3>
<ol>
<li>Teacher of the year in 2011</li>
```

```
<li>Coached the Boy's soccer team to the conference title in
2012</li>
<li>Three former students received prestigious scholarships in
2015</li>
</ol>
<h3> A brief Biography</h3>
<p> I am originally from Dallas, Tx.  I have many fond memories
of Dallas. Click <a
href="http://http://dallascityhall.com/Pages/default.aspx">here</
a> if you want to learn more about Dallas. </p>
</body>
</html>
```

Notice how we have embedded the link inside of the <p> tag. With links to remember that we not only need to add an address or link, but we also must indicate what text we want to display that will be linked. In this case, the word 'here' in the previous code will house the link and by clicking on that word, the visitor will be taken to that site. The other text will not be linked and will simply be placed around the linked text.

Now that we know how to add a link, let's explore a fun and useful way to add functionality for our visitors and make it easy for them to contact us. Let's add our email address as a link that visitors can click on to reach out to us in a convenient way. We will add this as the last element in our <head> section, right under the <h2> tag.

To add this functionality, you will build an element that looks very similar to a normal link element. However, you will add a command called "mailto:" that opens the visitor's email and generates a new email that is addressed to you. Here is an example of how it looks:

<a href="mailto:youremailaddress">Email Me</a>

You will notice the normal <a> tag for a link, for the href, we have added mailto: which is followed by an email address, and the link text at the end of the element before the closing tag. I will add the code below to my profile below the <h2> element at the bottom of the <head> section. Feel free to use your own email address where I have added the contact@learntoprogram.tv address.

We will place the <a> tags inside of <p> tags so that we can control their placement. In our opening <p> tag, we will add a center attribute to place it in the middle of the page.

Code Sample: Adding a new header and link

```
<p align="center"><a href="mailto:contact@learntoprogram.tv">
Email Me</a></p>
```

After adding that code, please save your code and then test it in the browser. The result should resemble this screenshot:

Figure 4-7—Screenshot of the current version of our site

Great work! Don't worry if it takes you a few tries. Learning to code takes considerable trial and error. However, it is the way that everyone learns. You can now add links and even allow your visitors to email you with one click of their mouse! That is certainly worth the effort it took.

Images: How to Make Your Site Picture Perfect!

Along with links, another cornerstone of every good site is images. The web is a highly visual medium. One of the best ways to add an engaging visual flair to your site is through the effective use of images. Good images help you to communicate messages, evoke emotion, and add additional layers of content to engage your audience.

When you'd like to add images to your site, you will use the <img> tag with a "src" attribute. The "src" stands for "Source" and works just like the <a> tag's "href" attribute. It tells the image tag where to find the image you'd want to include on your page.

Below is an example of a <img> tag. You will notice that it does not have a closing tag.

Code Sample: Example image tag

```
<img src="image url" alt="brief title of image" width="in pixels"
height="in pixels">
```

Let's explain the parts of this tag in more detail.

- <img will open your tag and element for adding images.

- src is short for source and directs the browser to where it will find an image.

- alt is what appears if there is an issue with displaying the image. It is also what will be read by a screen reader.

- Width will contain a number which will specify the width of the image (in pixels) that will be displayed.

  Height will contain a number which specify the height of the image (in pixels) that will be displayed.
- There are many options that can be used for images. However, you will want to always include these basic attributes in every

<img> tag. You want to tell the browser where to get the image, what text to place if it has an issue as well as the height and width.

There are two ways to source images for your site. Relative addressing tells your browser: "Look in our project folder for the file specified. Or, if a folder is specified, look within that folder for the file specified."

On the other hand, when we link to a source outside of our project, usually another website, it is referred to as an absolute address.

We will want to add a profile picture to the top of our site. Let's start with an example of a relative address and use an image that we already have.

At the top of our code, in the head section right below the <h2> tag and above the email address we just added, we will build our <img> tag so that we have a nice image at the top of our page. Go ahead and insert a blank <img> tag that looks just like the code sample below and we will add to it as we go.

Code Sample: Blank image tag

```
<img src="" alt="" width="" height="">
```

First, create a new subfolder on your computer inside of the folder you are saving your HTML to. This will be the folder we use to place our images.

To create a new folder, go to the folder where you are saving your HTML and CSS and right-click any blank area (or press CTRL +

click). This will create a pop-up menu from which you can select new folder.

Figure 5-1—Creating a new folder

Name your new folder "images".

In your folder, you should have an HTML file, a subfolder housing your CSS, and a subfolder with your images.

You now have a place to save any images that you want to display on your site. You can save a few images that you might want to add to your web project to this folder. For the purpose of this project, I will save images with a .jpg extension which indicates that they are JPEG files. Exploring image file types will not be discussed here. However, JPEG is a standard and widely used format that serves our purposes well. I recommend that you add some images and save them to the folder as JPEG files.

I have named my project folder My_Page and I am keeping my images in a folder titled images. To access that folder in an <img> tag, you can use a line of code like the code sample below. I have highlighted the src attribute pointing to the .jpeg file in our images folder.

Code Sample: Adding sizes to our image

```
<head>
        <title>My Page</title>

<link rel="stylesheet" type="text/css" href="css/style.css">
</head>
<body>
<h1>Thanks for visiting my page and learning more about me! </h1>

<h2>This site is designed as a personal profile.</h2>
<img src="images/headshot.jpg" alt="headshot" height="250"
width="200">
<p align="center"><a href="mailto:contact@learntoprogram.tv">
Email Me</a></p>
```

After adding the image, my site looks like this:

Figure 5-2—Current version of code after adding <img>

Don't worry if your image isn't centered above the email address! We will cover that soon.

We will now discuss how to add an image from another website. Please find an image online that you would like to use. To be able to use an image that is already online, you will need to locate that image address or url, and place that in your code. This a very simple process that is outlined below. First, put a blank image tag at the bottom of your code below the last <p> tag and right above the last </body> tag.

1. Navigate to the image you like

2. Right click your mouse button while hovering over the image

Figure 5-3—copying image address

3. Select "copy image address" from the menu that appears

4. Return to your code, and put your cursor between the quotes after src=

5. Right click on your mouse, and press paste.

You should now see the address in your <img> tag as part of the source attribute and you should mirror the following code sample.

Code Sample: Adding image from a url

```
<h3> A brief Biography</h3>
<p> I am originally from Dallas, Tx.  I have many fond memories
of Dallas. Click <a
href="http://http://dallascityhall.com/Pages/default.aspx">here</
a> if you want to learn more about Dallas.</p>
```

```
<img
src="http://images.freeimages.com/images/previews/67e/office-
1238353.jpg" alt="" width="" height="">
</body>
</html>
```

After adding the image, our site should resemble the following screen shot. Don't worry if yours is a different size. We will work on sizes soon. Here is how my page looks with the image.

Figure 5-4—with image from url added

Save your file and test your code in the browser.

This looks great! Adding images is a fun and creative way to layer in content and add depth to your ability to communicate with your visitors.

There are still a few elements that we need to add to our image tag. First, we have total control over the size of the image as it renders on our page, so let's work with our height and width. As you noticed when you rendered the latest version of your code, you do not need to enter a height and width. However, it is a best practice and something that you will want to have a good grasp of. Images will come in at different sizes due to their original properties. You will want to maintain control over the image, and make sure that you have prescribed a height and width that aligns with what you need for your page.

Default measurements are almost always in pixels or in numerical percentages in HTML5. As you get a feel for building web pages, you will frequently bounce back and forth between your code and the rendered version in your browser as you test different sizes. Not only is this OK, but it is also how professional and experienced developers work.

Coding is often a very iterative process filled with trial and error. You should be bouncing back and forth between your code and your rendered version in your browser. Embrace it and have fun knowing that is the best way to build something that you will ultimately be proud of. This is especially true when you are sizing things like images.

There are no absolute rules for sizes. It is similar to hanging pictures on the wall in your house. The first attempt is rarely perfect or exactly how you want it. Sizing images in HTML5 is very similar. Have fun trying out different options, take time to consider what works best, and always work towards a design and layout that is consistent with what you want to communicate.

While coding might be new for you, trust your instincts when it comes to final layout and design decisions. You know what your site should look like, and you will know it when you see it, so keep trying different options, tweak the code and test it often so that when you do see the layout that is perfect for you, you are confident because you have tried several.

I am going to add a width and height of 400 pixels or 200px to my img element. Please take some time to experiment with different sizes and test them in your browser.

Code Sample: Adding sizes to our image

```
<h3>A brief Biography</h3>
<p>I am originally from Dallas, Tx.  I have many fond memories of
Dallas. Click <a
href="http://http://dallascityhall.com/Pages/default.aspx">here</
a> if you want to learn more about Dallas.</p>
<img
src="http://images.freeimages.com/images/previews/67e/office-
1238353.jpg" alt="" width="400" height="400">
</body>
</html>
```

It is also necessary to add some text for our alt attribute. This text will appear if our image doesn't load. It is also what is read by a screen reader. Screen readers are software programs that allow blind or visually impaired users to read the text that is displayed on the computer screen with a speech synthesizer or braille display.

For my generic office image, I will add some basic text and will demonstrate it in the highlighted portion of the code sample below. Feel free to use whatever text that you feel briefly describes your image.

Code Sample: Adding alt text to an image

```
<h3>A brief Biography</h3>
<p>I am originally from Dallas, Tx.  I have many fond memories of
Dallas. Click <a
href="http://http://dallascityhall.com/Pages/default.aspx">here</
a> if you want to learn more about Dallas. </p>
<img
src="http://images.freeimages.com/images/previews/67e/office-
1238353.jpg" alt="My Office" width="400" height="400">
</body>
</html>
```

Take a moment to save your code and test it in the browser. As long as your image displays correctly, your alt text will not appear.

Finally, let's center our images. To do this, we will return to CSS. We will tell CSS to put the image on its own line and to take the full width of that line with an equal margin on either side. This can be accomplished with the rule below:

Code Sample: Centering our images

```
img {
    display: block;
    margin-left: auto;
    margin-right: auto;
}
```

Make sure that you save the CSS and HTML files and test them in the browser. They should now appear like this:

Figure 5-5—With images centered

You can have a lot of fun with images. A deeper understanding of CSS will provide you with even more creative options. It is important that you are learning the fundamentals through practice. This will give you a fantastic foundation for moving forward in your learning.

Tables: Additional organization and layout for your content

As we have discussed, HTML5 provides a great vehicle for structuring content for display on the web. Another common format you have access to is structuring data in tables.

As a part of our sample personal profile, we will put our most recent work history into a table similar to a common resume format. Here is an example of what we would like to finish with:

Figure 6-0—Example of data formatted in a table

Tables are a more complex element that require more lines of code than the other elements we have looked at. To learn how to build tables, will require several steps to build the table up as we master each step in the sequence.

The first step is to start a new page which will contain our work history. Here are the steps:

1. In Brackets, click on File

2. Click on New to open a new blank file.

3. Click on File again

4. Click on Save As

5. Name your file work.html and make sure when you save it that you have selected the folder called My_Page that contains the rest of our project. This is the same folder where we have saved our index.html file.

Here is the first block of code which will provide the basic table structure in HTML5. Start by adding the boilerplate. Title the page work history. We also want to make sure we add our CSS sheet. I have also correctly added the most recent position for our work history, which is as English Teacher at Lincoln High School which will start the formatting in a basic table structure.

Code Sample: Adding a basic table

```
<!DOCTYPE html>
<html>
<head>
<title>Work History</title>
<link rel="stylesheet" type="text/css" href="css/style.css">
</head>
<body>
<table>
<tr>
<td>English Teacher</td>
```

```
<td>Lincoln High School</td>
<td>2015-2016</td>
</tr>
</table>
</body>
</html>
```

Similar to the way that all of the items in a list were housed between two <li> tags, all of the elements in a table will live between an opening <table> and a closing </table> tag.

The <tr> tag is short for table row. This tag separates each unique row. Each item listed between <tr> tags will occupy a cell and the items will be organized horizontally into rows.

Each item between a <td> tag will occupy its own cell and represents the data in your table.

The code in the preceding sample should render a one row table that looks like this:

Figure 6-1—First steps in building a table

The table thus far is incomplete. However, it is important that this first block of code is accurate. It should provide a good sense of the pattern we will use to build the rest of the table.

I am now going to add two more blocks of code just like the last sample. Each of these blocks will represent one row of employment history and follow the exact same pattern. Here is the full code sample:

Code Sample: Adding a basic table

```
<table>
<tr>
<td>English Teacher</td>
<td>Lincoln High School</td>
<td>2015-2016</td>
</tr>
<tr>
<td>Soccer Coach</td>
<td>Lincoln High School</td>
<td>2012-2015</td>
</tr>
<tr>
<td>Tutor</td>
<td>Rosedale High School</td>
<td>2010-2011</td>
</tr>
</table>
```

We now have three rows of employment history in our table. Let's save our file, and test it in the browser. It should look like this:

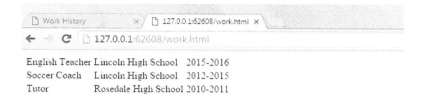

English Teacher Lincoln High School   2015-2016
Soccer Coach   Lincoln High School   2012-2015
Tutor   Rosedale High School 2010-2011

Figure 6-2—Example of data formatted in a table

So far, so good! But we aren't done yet! A good table should be designed with good headers so that our visitors know exactly what they are looking at.

To add our headers, we will simply add an opening <thead> tag, and then create a new row with our <tr> tags containing the header for each column. We will then add a closing </thead> tag. We also need to place the body of the table in between an opening <tbody> tag and a closing </tbody> tag. The code block for our table is shown below. I have highlighted where we want to insert our header code and what I have placed there.

Code Sample: Adding Table headers

```
<table>
<thead>
<tr>
<th>Title</th>
<th>Location</th>
```

```
<th>Year</th>
</tr>

</thead>
<tbody>
<tr>
<td>English Teacher</td>
<td>Lincoln High School</td>
<td>2015-2016</td>
</tr>
<tr>
<td>Soccer Coach</td>
<td>Lincoln High School</td>
<td>2012-2015</td>
</tr>
<tr>
<td>Tutor</td>
<td>Rosedale High School</td>
<td>2010-2011</td>
</tr>
</tbody>
</table>
```

Our table is certainly getting there! Let's save the file and render it in a browser.

Figure 6-3—Example of data formatted in a table

At this point, the basic structure of our table is taking shape. We will want to add some basic styling to our table. A good table should have a simple and well organized layout. It is very important not to overdo it. However, by adding some borders and emphasizing certain text and rows, we can visually help our visitors understand the data in our table and make sure that the information flows logically.

To better separate the data, we will add a border. A border is optional, but we will add one here to help you practice with its functionality. We will also add an attribute to control the width of the table.

Code Sample: Adding border and width to a table

```
<table border="1" style="width:100%">
<thead>
<tr>
<th>Title</th>
<th>Location</th>
<th>Year</th>
```

```
</tr>
</thead>
```

You will notice the width is set to 100%. The two most common options for sizing in HTML5 are either in pixels or percentages. Save your file, test your code and see how the table looks at 100%.

I am going to set the final version at 50%. I have highlighted it in the code sample that is shown below. We will also center our table with another attribute in the opening <table> tag. We will add an align attribute with a property of center.

The last step is to add an overall title to our table. In HTML5, this is referred to as our caption. We will add an opening <caption> tag and a closing </caption> tag and place the text between the tags we want to use as a title for our table. You can see where to place it from the sample below. The code we are adding is highlighted.

Code Sample: Adding border, width and alignment to a table

```
<table border="1" style="width:50%" align="center">
<caption>My Work History</caption>
<thead>
```

I also would like to move the image of the office we added to the last page. It is located below the <h2> on our index page.

To cut and paste your code:

1. Highlight the code you want. In this case, it is the entire <img> tag.
2. Right click while it is highlighted.
3. Click on Cut

4. Return to your work.html file
5. Place your cursor on a new line below the caption tag
6. Right click
7. Click paste

Here is the code from the head portion of our table with a border, width, title and center alignment added and the img tag from the toehr file we that we just cut and pasted. In this step, we will also want to add an <h1> which you can view in the highlighted portion.

   Code Sample: Adding border, width and alignment to a table

```
<table border="1" style="width:50%" align="center">
<caption>My Work History</caption>
<img
src="http://images.freeimages.com/images/previews/67e/office-
1238353.jpg" alt="My office" width="400" height="200">
<thead>
<tr>
<th>Title</th>
<th>Location</th>
<th>Year</th>
</tr>
</thead>
```

When we test our code in the browser, it should look like this:

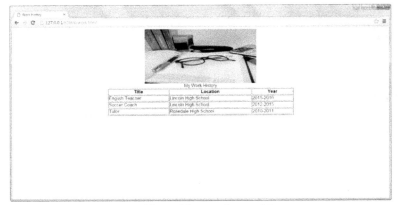

Figure 6-4—Our page with a table, caption and image

We will also want a centered header for our page. I am going to add the following <h1> tag to our page. I have highlighted the portion I am adding.

Code Sample: Adding border, width and alignment to a table

```
<h1 align="center">Welcome to my work history page!</h1>
<table border="1" style="width:50%" align="center">
<caption>My Work History</caption>
<img
src="http://images.freeimages.com/images/previews/67e/office-
1238353.jpg" alt="My office" width="400" height="200">
```

Our titles and headers might need some additional styling to provide a proper visual hierarchy to our table. In order to do this, we will return to CSS and add some rules to ensure that we format and style our table exactly the way we want to.

Open the CSS file that we started earlier in your text editor. If you recall, we had added one rule to style our header. Our CSS should appear like this when we open it.

Code Sample: Current status of CSS code

```
h1 {
    color: blue;
}

body {
    font-family:  Arial, Helvetica, sans-serif

}

img {
    display: block;
    margin-left: auto;
    margin-right: auto;
}
```

CSS rules start with a selector, which is the element we are adding styling to. They contain a property, which indicates what we are going to add, and the value with provides the exact nature of the styling.

To add visual cues to our table, I would like to make the caption the biggest text size. I need to add prominence to our headers so that the text from this portion stands out. To do this, I will add three CSS rules. Here is the code:

Code Sample: Adding CSS rules for our table

```
caption {
    font-size: 30px
```

```
}
th {
    font-size: 24px
}
tbody {
    color:blue;
    font-size: 20px
}
```

We should now have a larger title, prominent headers, and blue text in our table. Save your CSS file, switch back to the work.html file, press Live Preview and test it in the browser. As a tip, Live Preview only works when your editor is open to an .html file.

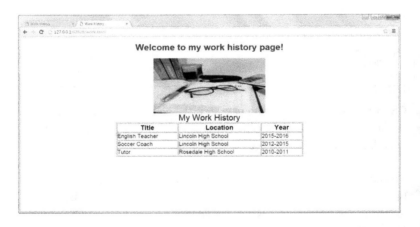

Figure 6-7—Table with our CSS added

Fantastic job! The table looks great and is worthy of the hard earned work experience it communicates.

Now that we have learned some very effective ways of displaying content on multiple pages, it is time to build an important feature to support the overall visitor experience which is navigation.

Navigation: Linking your pages together

Now that you are creating multiple pages, we need to add the ability to move back and forth between the pages.

Navigation bars are one element of your page that can get highly stylized. For our purposes here, we will aim for a very simple implementation to give us navigational functionality and to allow us a base to build upon that can be used for our future learning.

The navigation bar will live at the top of our HTML document. Our goal is to list links to other pages so that visitors can go back and forth. In a simple way, we are adding links to a specific part of our page.

We will use opening <nav> and closing </nav> tags with our links nesting inside of them.

Later, we will be adding a blog page, so I will go ahead and add that page to the nav element in order to save time later.

 You should now insert the following code into the <body> section of your main page. I have highlighted the section to add.

Code Sample: Adding navigation links

```
<head>
        <title>My Page</title>

<link rel="stylesheet" type="text/css" href="css/styling.css">
```

```
</head>
<body>
<nav>
  <a href="blog.html">My Blog</a> |
  <a href="work.html">Work History</a> |
</nav>

<h1 align="center">Thanks for visiting my page and learning more
about me! </h1>
```

You should now save your file and test it in the browser. When you test
it, click on the Work History link, and it should take you to that page.
The My Blog link will not work until we create the page in the next
exercise.

Figure 7-1—With navigation links added

You should now open your new work.html file. Insert the highlighted
code below into the same section of that page.

Code Sample: Adding navigation links

```
<head>
        <title>Work History</title>

<link rel="stylesheet" type="text/css" href="css/styling.css">
</head>
<body>
<nav>
  <a href="mypage.html">Main Page</a> |
  <a href="blog.html">My Blog</a> |
</nav>

<h1 align="center">Welcome to my work history page</h1>
```

Save your file and test your code. It should render in the upper left and the link to the Main Page should be live. We will create the Blog page in the next section. As you study the code, you can see that what we are doing is adding links to our own pages inside of <nav> tags. Here is a screen shot:

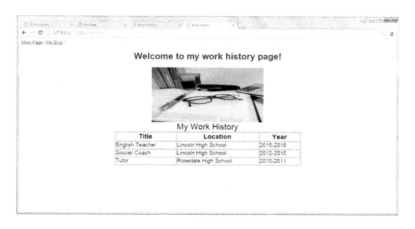

Figure 7-2—work.html page with navigation links added

Great work! Allowing for easy and functional navigation is the key to a positive user experience. You should now see how to begin to use a fundamental understanding of different elements to speed your learning in other areas. In this case, a knowledge of how to format tags and links assisted us in quickly learning navigation. A key to good programming is to constantly "borrow" what you know in one area, and to apply it as often as it makes sense in other areas.

Now that we are adding multiple ways for visitors to experience our content, it is time to add some important interactive elements and allow our visitors to provide us data and feedback through the use of forms.

Forms: Add Additional Interactivity

Forms are a great addition to your site. They offer another layer of communication with your visitors. Good forms allow you to accept feedback and data from your visitors. As a result, your website becomes an effective two way street between you and your guests. To properly store and use this data on the backend, you will need to add some additional code and programming (not covered here). We will show you how to add a basic form on the front end of a website. This will help you to understand the fundamentals of presenting forms in a browser and begin to think about all of the fantastic ways you can add this interactive feature to your site.

For this example, we are going to create a new blog on our site, but we want to ask for some information from our visitors about what type of blog they want to see. We will build a form to collect this information from our visitors. In order to maximize your learning, we will build three different types of small forms.

The first step is to create a new file in your text editor and call it blog.html. Save it in the My_Page folder that we are using for our project. This is the same process you followed to create the work.html file in the last section.

Add the following code to the top of the blank file to get your HTML file started with a <head> section, your navigation elements and the content that we will use to explain the purpose of this page. You will then link your CSS file. Take a minute to study the elements in this code. They should all be familiar to you. You can also review what was covered in previous sections of the book.

Code Sample: Starting our page to house our forms

```
<!DOCTYPE HTML>
<html>
<head>
        <title>My Blog</title>

<link rel="stylesheet" type="text/css" href="css/styling.css">
</head>
<body>
<nav>
  <a href="mypage.html">Main Page</a> |
  <a href="work.html">Work History</a> |
</nav>

<h1 align="center">My Blog Is Coming Soon! </h1>

<h2>Help me start my blog!!</h2>

<p>I plan on starting a blog very soon. I plan on writing about
my favorite topics which include education, teaching, and web
design.  Will you help me? Feel free to let me know which topics
you would prefer, and send me your personal information so I can
```

```
add you to my mailing list and let you know when the posts begin.
Thanks again for your help, I look forward to hearing from
you!</p>

</body>
</html>
```

There are many options to design and style forms in HTML and CSS. I have chosen a simple framework that will group different elements together and automatically add some borders to keep our forms neat and organized.

We are going to introduce a few new tags, which will be used in the code sample below.

- The <form> tag acts as a container for all of our form elements.

- The <br> tag is short for break. It will help us to separate elements onto different lines.

- The <fieldset> tag will group our elements. This is not a required part of a form, but it will help us to separate and group elements from a design perspective. As you try out different approaches with your code, feel free to comment out these tags and see how the form renders without the fieldset tag. This tag will default to a width of 100% if you do not indicate a size. We can use either a % or pixels.

- The <legend> tag provides a title for a particular section of a form.

- The <input> tag is used to declare what type of input this section of the form will accept through the type attribute. In this first instance, it will be type= "radio" for radio buttons. Later in the form, we will also use text.

The code sample below provides the first section of our form. We will create three radio buttons to allow visitors to "vote" for what topics they want to read about on our blog; education, web design, or both.

Code Sample: First block of code for our forms

```
<form>
  <h3>I would love to hear from you!</h3>
  <br>
  <fieldset style="width:50%">
  <legend> What type of topics would you like to see
discussed?</legend>
  <input type="radio" name="blogtype" value="education">Education
  <br>
  <input type="radio" name="blogtype" value="web">Web Design
  <br>
  <input type="radio" name="blogtype" value="both">Both!
  <br>
  </fieldset>
```

The value attribute associates the value given by the input. The name attribute is an entry that indicates the data you are collecting. The name attribute is used to reference elements later in Javascript, or to reference form data after a form is submitted, both of which are beyond our scope here. It is important to understand these other uses in order to later use advanced skills like Javascript. The now important to have a good understanding of the building blocks in HTML.

You can see in the text what will appear in the form that renders in the browser. At the end of each line of code that begins with an input type, you can see the words Education, Web Design, and Both!. Whatever text is outside of the <input> tag will appear in the browser.

After each line, we also added a <br> to help us space our form elements.

The next sample of code will provide another group of form elements. However, these will be text field inputs instead of radio buttons.

Code Sample: First block of code for our forms

```
<fieldset style="width:50%">
<legend> Your Information</legend>
 First name:<br>
<input type="text" name="firstname">
 <br>
 Last name:<br>
 <input type="text" name="lastname">
 <br>
 Email:<br>
 <input type="email" name="email">
<br>
 Zip Code:<br>
 <input type="number" name="number">
 <br>
 </fieldset>
```

Before starting to work with this code, you should spend a few minutes comparing the two samples in order to determine similarities and differences. The tags are primarily the same. The main differences are the values in the attributes. It is important to remember that we are now adding a form that accepts text inputs while the previous form was a series of radio buttons.

You will also notice we placed the breaks between the text and the input fields. This was an optional design choice. You can place your <br> tags wherever you'd like. If you want the text input fields to appear next to the text like in the radio button section, just switch the <br> tags to after the input fields like we did with the radio button section.

After adding the code, please save your file and test your code in a browser. It should look like this:

Figure 8-1—First form elements added

Our last section of code will provide our visitors with an open entry text box to send us their own comments, thoughts and ideas. Instead of specific inputs, we want to set up a text box with a general question and/or title so that visitors can type and submit their thoughts.

In this last sample of code, you will also see a <textarea> tag. You will open and close this tag as normal. This creates the text box. You will need to indicate a size by selecting a number of rows and columns.

Before the closing </form> tag you will also see an <input> tag with an attribute of type="submit". This creates a generic submit button for our users to send us their information which will live at the bottom of our form. In this block, we will also close our form, body and html tags.

Code Sample: First block of code for our forms

```
<fieldset style="width:35%">
<legend>Feel free to add your ideas about future blog
posts:</legend>
<textarea rows="5" columns="500"></textarea>
</fieldset>
<br><br>
<input type="submit" value="Submit">

</form>
</body>
```

Save your code and test it on the browser. It should appear like this:

Figure 1-10—With text box added

You now have an excellent foundational understanding of forms. We have built three different types of forms, and cleanly laid them out inside of one form with a submit button. Great work! This will allow you to have fun as you learn other technologies in the future. It will enable you to create additional styling in CSS and interactivity in Javascript to work with the data you receive from visitors and to further enrich their experience.

Next Steps

You certainly have much to be proud of in completing this book and all of the exercises we covered. I truly believe that when it comes to coding, learning by doing is the only meaningful way to learn. We have certainly gotten a lot of practice. Congratulations!

Beyond that, I think building web pages should be fun. I will also improve your ability to connect and to communicate with wider audiences. I encourage you to build on what you have learned here and to use it as a springboard to continue your learning.

You now know the basics of how to add content on the World Wide Web. You also understand the tags, elements and attributes that will allow you to work with that content. You can now learn how to style that content with CSS which will make your web designs come to life with color and creativity. You can also learn Javascript which is the language that allows for deeper levels of interactivity on the web. It enables greater communication with the user and browser to make your web elements more dynamic.

Just think about how much you have learned.=You have only just started! In the future, you will only be limited by your own dedication and imagination.

Onward!

Online Courses from LearnToProgram

Become a Certified Web Developer Level One

Become a Certified Web Developer Level Two

Certified Mobile Developer

Roadmap to Web Developer

HTML and CSS for Beginners (with HTML5

Javascript for Beginners

Programming for Absolute Beginners

PHP and MySQL for Beginners

jQuery for Beginners

CSS Development with CSS3

Node.js for Beginners

Advanced Javascript Development

AJAX Development

SQL Database for Beginners

Ruby on Rails for Beginners

Famo.us Javascript Framework

GitHub Fundamentals

Creating a PHP Login Script

Front End Developer with Adobe Dreamweaver

Codeless Web Development with Adobe Muse

Mobile App Development with HTML5

10 Apps in 10 Weeks

Java Programming for Beginners

Swift Language Fundamentals

iOS Development for Beginners

Android Development for Beginners

10 Apps in 10 Weeks: iOS Edition

Python for Beginners

Construct 2 for Beginners

Game Development with Unity

Mobile Game Development for iOS

3D Fundamentals with iOS

Project Management using Microsoft Project

.Net for Beginners

C++ for Beginners

Joomla for Beginners

User Experience Design Fundamentals

Photoshop CS6 Training for Coders

Design for Coders

C Programming for Beginners

Objective C for Beginners

Introduction to Web Development

Game Development Fundamentals with Python